Love Is Funny, Love Is Sad

Books by Ben Milder

POETRY

The Good Book Says . . . : Light Verse to Illuminate the Old
Testament (1995)

The Good Book Also Says . . . : Numerous Humorous Poems
Inspired by the New Testament (1999)

Love Is Funny, Love Is Sad (2002)

MEDICAL

The Fine Art of Prescribing Glasses Without Making a Spectacle
of Yourself (1979)

HISTORY

On the Shoulders of Giants: A History of Ophthalmology at
Washington University (1999)

Love Is Funny, Love Is Sad

Poems by

Ben Milder

TIME BEING BOOKS
POETRY IN SIGHT AND SOUND

An imprint of Time Being Press
St. Louis, Missouri

Time Being Books
10411 Clayton Road
St. Louis, Missouri 63131

Time Being Books is an imprint of Time Being Press
St. Louis, Missouri

Time Being Press is a 501(c)(3) not-for-profit corporation.

Time Being Books volumes are printed on acid-free paper, and binding materials are chosen for strength and durability.

ISBN 1-56809-078-1 (Paperback)

Library of Congress Cataloging-in-Publication Data:

Milder, Benjamin, 1915–
    Love is funny, love is sad / by Ben Milder.
        p. cm. — (Poetry in sight and sound)
    ISBN 1-56809-078-1 (pbk. : alk. paper)
    1. Love poetry, American. I. Title. II. Series.

    PS3563.I37159 L68 2002
    811'.54 — dc21

                                                              2002070345

Manufactured in the United States of America

First Edition, first printing (2002)

Acknowledgments

It is a pleasure to acknowledge, with thanks, the invaluable contributions of Jerry Call, Managing Editor of Time Being Books, Sheri Vandermolen, Editor in Chief, and Louis Daniel Brodsky in the preparation of this volume.

My thanks to the editors of the following publications, in which several of these poems have appeared: *International Journal of Computers and Mathematics* ("The Golem"); *Journal of Irreproducible Results* ("I Wish I Were an Analyst"); *Light* ("The Lady Next Door" and "The Terrible Tyrannosaurus"); *Optometric Economics* ("*La ronde*"); and *Pharos* ("Sex Appeal").

For Jeanne,

without whose love and encouragement
this collection of meanderings
through the highways and byways of love
could not have materialized

Contents

Love Is Sad

Epilogue

Love Is Funny,
Love Is Sad

Foreword

Love has many faces, wears many masks. As we move from childhood into adult life, love is exciting, exhilarating. We do crazy things in its name. Love is, in many ways, funny.

Before long, we are into middle age, with its problems, its insecurities. Love becomes enmeshed in uncertainties about our libidos, our fading dreams, our future. It is a time of stark reality, a time for reflection, often a time of sadness, even depression.

In the twilight of our years, confronted with the inevitable end, we look back and realize that love does not disappear, rather, remains in the tenderness and caring that are the essence of mature love. And although we can still find something humorous about love, it is more likely to be dark humor than frivolous.

The poems in this collection reflect my endeavors through the years to stay afloat on the shifting tides of love.

Ben Milder

Love Is Funny

SEX AND LOVE

The Lady Next Door

I'm in love with the lady next door.
It's a feeling I just can't ignore.
        Though it sounds idiotic,
        All my dreams are rhapsodic.
I have never felt this way before.

In the warmth of her friendship to bask,
I'd do anything that she might ask —
        Fight a dragon, a beast,
        Resurrect the deceased —
I would meet any challenge or task.

Yes, I swear on the stars up above,
I would go to all lengths for her love —
        Cut the grass, shovel snow
        When it's thirty below.
We were destined to fit, hand in glove.

I'm in love with the lady next door.
For her, I'd do things I abhor —
        Brush my teeth after meals,
        Wash her automobiles —
If she'd only be mine. Furthermore,

I would marry the lady next door,
But I fear it would cause an uproar.
        Though I've made that suggestion,
        It is out of the question,
'Cause I'm twelve, and she's seventy-four.

The Terrible Tyrannosaurus

From a 1992 news report:

*Fossil remains of a tyrannosaurus
found in a Wisconsin quarry*

How the terrible tyrannosaurus,
Which roamed the earth eons before us,
      Though colossal and feared
      Nonetheless disappeared
Is a story unlikely to bore us.

It has paleontologists guessing
How an animal so prepossessing,
      So huge and carnivorous,
      Is gone (saints deliver us!).
It's a question that's well worth addressing.

Though our planet they're no longer gracing,
In my head, one wild thought keeps on racing:
      If you'll just close your eyes,
      Can you visualize
Two tyrannosauri embracing?

Although modesty seems to forbid it,
It all comes down to sex, let's admit it.
      Those Brobdingnagian males,
      With their fifteen-foot tails,
Make me wonder just how they did it.

If the act of sex they were renouncin',
Then those fossil remains in Wisconsin
      Which were found in a quarry
      Were tyrannosauri
Who should have read Masters and Johnson.

Sex and Love

Sex and love!
Sex and love!
One-syllable words that should go hand-in-glove.
Suppose you should lose one
Or you had to choose one.
Which one would it be? Would it be sex or love?

Sex is inviting!
Sex is exciting!
But sex is no hardy perennial.
You're up to the hilt in it,
But then it starts wiltin'; it
Soon goes from white-hot to merely congenial.

Love, in rebuttal,
Is often more subtle.
It quietly sneaks up. There's nowhere to hide.
You feel great, you feel mizz'able,
But love is invisible.
You can't wash it off. It's embedded inside.

But there's one way to cash in
On both love and passion
When the urge to have both is acute.
It quite simply is this:
Try connubial bliss.
The question would then become moot.

Anabolic Steroids

If, in the hay, you'd like to frolic
In a setting that's bucolic
And you employ drugs anabolic

'Cause you don't like the status quo,
You can help your muscles grow,
But there will be a quid pro quo.

E.g., there's all that scuttlebutt
About the side effects, which shut
Your sex drive down to just a putt.

Suppose you've spent your last simoleon
On drugs that they call "metabolian,"
And you still look something like Napoleon,

And your girlfriend's dreams still seem to plague her,
About you as Arnold Schwarzenegger.
There might be other ways to snag her.

With exercise, you still can muscle up,
But time is short; you'd better hustle up
If it's your aim to get her bustle up!

How Does Your Garden Grow?

There's acupuncture, but, additional,
There are those drugs they call "traditional,"
And the Chinese find no impropriety
In herbs of every variety.

Strange concoctions from bears' claws
Would give the average patient pause,
And things made from the sting of bees
Are said to mitigate disease.

But the favorite item they're dispensing
Is an Oriental root, the ginseng.
It looks a great deal like horseradish,
And for centuries, it has been faddish.

It captures the imagination
With its claim to aid rejuvenation,
But it's honored mostly in the breach,
'Cause those roots are sold for two grand each!

The Orientals have a credo:
"There's naught too good for your libido."
But in the U.S., no one lacks
For cheaper aphrodisiacs.

The Golem

When man created the computer,
It was not female, male, or neuter.
And from the day of its creation,
It went about its automation,
In all its automated splendor,
Without a thought as to its gender.

It was, at one time, my intention
That I could further this invention
By making it my own Pygmalion.
And though its languages were alien
And it might balk and lisp and stammer,
It would become its own programmer.

What's more, it would have the incentive
Of being even more inventive
And, with its newfound human qualities,
Indulge in some of life's frivolities.

Forgoing programs academian
For life that's somewhat more Bohemian,
It might eschew the intellectual
And have a fling at things more sexual.

But computers rarely make apology
For inherent flaws in their technology,
So this one's plan for warmth and amity
Was bound to end up in calamity,

Because thrown upon its own resources
And unaware what intercourse is,
When it programmed what it thought was wooing,
Its floppy disks proved its undoing.

LOVE IS A CINDER
IN THE EYE OF THE BEHOLDER

Limerick #16

A spinster named Alice Magruder
Prayed each night, on her knees, for a suitor,
    A compatible gent
    Of marital bent
Or at least an attractive intruder.

La ronde

Off to grammar school she goes,
With spectacles upon her nose,
Neither conscious of nor caring
About the glasses she is wearing.

Then she moves into her teens;
Parents all know what that means:
At the first suggestion of a bust,
Contact lenses are a "must."

The facts of life, mom will explain now.
Braces go right down the drain now.
The braces, yes, have bit the dust,
But contact lenses are a "must."

With teenage boys, she starts to mingle;
Sans contacts, she would still be single.
The preacher says, "Dost thou . . ." — she dost!
Those lenses must have fueled her lust.

Children come, and it's chaotic.
She learns the meaning of "neurotic."
The contact lenses, once a "must,"
Lie in a drawer, just gathering dust.

At last, the end. She's laid to rest,
With folded hands across her chest.
Into those hands someone has thrust
Those contact lenses, once a "must,"

And we remain behind, unknowing
If she'll need those lenses where she's going.

Gloria Gonzalez

Palm Beach Post, 4/14/92:

> *A county judge will hear arguments on a motion to dismiss a case against Gloria Gonzalez, whose bikini-clad bottom got her arrested earlier this year for violating a county ordinance regulating street vendors and their attire.*

9/15/92:

> *Judge's decision: Hot dog vendor can wear thong in public.*

As I lollygagged over my coffee and toast,
I suddenly found myself deeply engrossed
In a story displayed on page one of the *Post*.

The case on the docket: one frankfurter vendor.
This time, the offender was feminine gender.
Why did the police at the scene apprehend her?

The officers, Jones and McCarthy (the meanies),
In court, testified that the girl who sold weenies
Was clad in the smallest of minibikinis.

"With her working attire little more than a thong
And with customers lined up at least four blocks long,
We thought that just possibly something was wrong.

"The hot dog we'd bought, we had scarcely digested,
When we noted Gonzalez was nearly bare-chested,
And we felt it our duty that she be arrested."

The county attorney, at this point, arose:
"In presenting the case for our side, we propose
To prove the defendant wore almost no clothes.

"Because the bikini was just itty-bitty,
That girl is a blemish upon our fair city,
And therefore, Your Honor should show her no pity."

"OK," said the judge, "it appears that you base
Your plea that the outfit's a public disgrace.
Well, you've had your say. Now sit down; rest your case."

The defendant's attorney then rose, as requested.
He stated, "Your Honor, we do not contest it.
In Gloria's work clothes, she's almost bare-chested.

"Judge, that's a fact that we do not dispute;
The bikini, it's true, was no more than minute.
But the state's implications, we rise to refute.

"Her quality hot dogs were what men were buying,
And her pickles and relish were most satisfying.
But her buns were outstanding, there is no denying.

"Put yourself, if you will, in the lady's position:
In a business where there is severe competition,
She behaved in the very best business tradition.

"The girl's business genius is our chief defense.
She displayed her best assets — the hot dogs — and, hence,
We request that the court sample our evidence.

"If the judge will agree to take one little bite
Of the hot dogs in question, our case is airtight.
It's the frank, not the girl, that whets one's appetite."

"The judge said, "I'll now rule on what that first bite meant.
Although the bikini may cause some excitement,
Her buns are the reason to quash the indictment.

"Will Gloria Gonzalez, defendant, please rise?
We've noted just how you display merchandise.
In this court's opinion, that's free enterprise!

"Since most hot-dog lovers would not stigmatize you,
It would be unjust in our eyes to chastise you.
In fact, in all likelihood, we'll patronize you.

"And so, having noshed, the indictment is quashed!"

The Pearly Gates

At the Pearly Gates stood Mr. Pettit.
Said St. Peter, "I truly regret it,
      But we can't let you in,
      For you've committed no sin;
The pure life — you seem to have led it.

"Admission to Heaven is meant for
All sinners. That's whom we have sent for.
      Since you don't need redemption,
      We can make no exemption.
You've done nothing that you need repent for.

"Go back to Earth, Pettit, and send us
Some proof you've done something horrendous.
      Any wrong you've committed
      Can get you admitted,
Any sin, either small or tremendous.

"Those profligate sinners who've spurned
Redemption are sure to be burned,
      But you can be saved
      If you're a wee bit depraved.
Just ring the bell when you've returned."

Said Pettit, "That's quite a high price,
But since it's St. Peter's advice,
      Though it isn't my style,
      I must sin for a while
So I can enter into Paradise."

Back to Earth went our hero, to sin,
Though he wasn't sure where to begin.
      Nonetheless, sin he must,
      Be it stealing or lust
Or temptations like gambling and gin.

Soon, a lady appeared in the distance,
Whose words lowered Pettit's resistance:
      "I am starved for affection
      From any direction."
Pettit said, "May I be of assistance?"

So that was the lady he went for.
(He suspected that she had been sent for!)
    He plunged in with fervor,
    Which, to an observer,
Was something that he could repent for.

Though at first he was not interested,
He did what St. Peter suggested.
    As she squealed with delight
    Through most of the night,
He explained, "I am just being tested.

"But, alas, I must now take my leave,
Because I'm here merely on a reprieve."
    But she cried, "We're not done yet!
    We haven't begun yet!
I have several more tricks up my sleeve."

"No. To the Pearly Gates I must proceed.
I have sinned. For forgiveness I'll plead."
    But she said, "You can't enter
    Those gates as repenter,
For in my eyes, you've done a good deed."

One Night in Valdosta

You'll weep at this tale of how two lovers lost a
Lot more than just sleep, from one night in Valdosta.
She whispered, "This motel's ground floor's too exposed,
So please, dear, be sure that the curtains are closed."

And having divested themselves of their garments,
They embarked on . . . let's call it an all-star performance,
With diversions and quirks that were unprecedented
And games Kama Sutra could not have invented.

"Do you hear that strange sound, dear," he asked when they paused,
"A muffled staccato that sounds like applause?
It couldn't be thunder, for the sky's clear, I'm certain."
"But you can't see the sky, dear, if you closed the curtain."

They turned toward the window, the source of the sound.
He blanched and she let out a shriek when they found
The drapes he was sure he had fastened completely
Were fastened, regrettably, not very neatly.

Through a gap of six inches, six faces were peering.
From the looks on those faces, they seemed to be cheering.
Twelve eyes stared, unblinking, in sheer fascination,
Six pairs of hands meeting in silent ovation.

Now comes the part that will have you all weeping.
At this hour in Valdosta, most people are sleeping.
Along comes a sheriff to admonish the crowd
That loitering in Valdosta at night's not allowed.

Then into the window the sheriff is peering,
And he sees at a glance what had the crowd cheering.
He says, while his face to the window is fastened,
"Being nude in Valdosta is something you dasn't!"

He turns to the crowd. "Please go home. This is frightful."
But they cry, "We can't leave yet. It's all too delightful.
There's ne'er been a spectacle with such panache in."
"Get lost," says the cop. "That gal's nude, and he's flashin'."

Next morning, in court, they are properly clad.
Judge Brown wears a frown. He intones, "This looks bad."
"But it's those peeping Toms," says the pair. "They're at fault,"
Which plea the judge takes with a large grain of salt.

"So it's *mucho* dinero or the slammer for you."
"Does the court accept VISA?" The judge says, "I do."
So what started out pleasantly in the end cost a
Whole lot of cash, for one night in Valdosta!

Londonderry Air

The Brits said, "She's so musical.
You can see it in her face."
But I'm certain that her face would stop a clock.
Her smile revealed no Gershwin;
Of Puccini, there's no trace,
And she didn't make me think of Strauss or Bach.

No music, yet I turned my head,
Afraid that I had missed it,
And still no trace of Debussy's *La Mer*.
But then I saw her from the rear,
And, as the Brits insisted,
There was music in her London derrière.

The Clock

This tale involves a scheme most shoddy
By a lady with a luscious body.
It's true that I took certain chances,
But her response to my advances

Was a plan to wreck my sleeping hours
With a gift: a clock with awesome powers,
A clock designed to take my measure,
Wreaking vengeance at her pleasure.

The act of sex is now a fiction.
The clock's become my sole addiction.
I hide it underneath my bed,
To drown its raucous din. Instead,

Just like a carillon it rings,
Resonating with the springs,
A particularly shabby tactic
Just when things should be climactic.

I shot at it and stomped and hit it.
Once, in a rage, I even bit it.
I've practiced every sort of crime on it,
Yet somehow, I can still tell time on it.

Distraught, I sought and found the donor,
Explained that I had made a boner,
Apologized if I offended,
And hoped the episode was ended.

Despite the urge to hurl a bomb at her,
I handed back the smashed chronometer
And fled from its tintinnabulation,
To a welcome somnolent vacation.

HANKY-PANKY

Quiche

Sam said, "Waitress, a steak and gin rickey."
And Mickey said, "I'd like a quickie."
      She said, "I'm no trollop"
      And fetched him a wallop,
Which explains his black eye and big hickey.

Said Sam, "In your manner of speech,
I'm afraid you've committed a breach.
      When you said to that chickie,
      'May I have a *quickie*,'
I think you pronounce that word *keesh*."

Love Thy Neighbor

Matthew 22:39

You shall love your neighbor as yourself.

What Matthew here advises
Could be fraught with dire surprises.
And that verse must come as something of a shock,
For if I love myself, I find
I must be similarly inclined
Toward every single neighbor on my block.

Though those words could not be clearer,
As I look into the mirror
And my image beckons me, just like Narcissus,
I can sense there's trouble brewing.
Will that verse be my undoing,
'Cause I shall have to love my neighbor's missus?

What a sad dilemma this is.
If I love my neighbor's missus
(For after all, she is my neighbor too),
I am sure I'd love her madly,
Which she, of course, would suffer gladly
And which her husband's apt to misconstrue.

To avoid the consequences,
I shall have to mend some fences
If I pursue that chapter and that verse,
'Cause if I don't come to my senses,
The existing evidence is
I shall end up with two broken legs or worse!

Let's Toast the Most

On Independence Day, this year,
Despite the hour's lateness,
Let's toast the great names we revere
And pay homage to their greatness.

There's John Paul Jones, who loved to fight,
And Alexander Graham Bell.
There's Edison, who gave us light,
And Truman, who just gave us hell.

There's JFK and FDR
And other great politicos.
There's Henry Ford and his first car
And the guy who gave us pantyhose.

We think of Whitney's cotton gin,
De Forest and his TV tubes,
Of Longfellow's "Evangeline,"
And Raquel Welch's famous boobs.

But the one to whom we owe the most,
A nameless, long-forgotten Yankee —
We raise our glasses now to toast
The man who gave us "hanky-panky."

Après Pro

Concerning all sports, my wife's been apathetic.
She's now into tennis; in fact, she's frenetic.
How did she become, all at once, so athletic?

She discovered that backhands and drop shots and slices
And other more intricate tennis devices
Are taught by our new pro — at staggering prices.

He's six feet three inches and lean as a splinter.
He covers the court like an Olympic sprinter.
And guess who's supporting him all through the winter?

He's young, and he's handsome (at least his moustache is).
The ladies, en masse, have postponed their hot flashes.
That pro is no dummy; he knows where the cash is.

He runs the pro shop, where the clothes are all current.
My wife's in there daily, though I wish that she weren't.
Her clothes racks are loaded, but that's no deterrent.

She has Fila, Adidas, et al. in her closet.
The pro extends credit, but she overdraws it.
I'm broke. Could I just leave her as a deposit?

Good heavens! That idea was not mine, or was it?

The Brown-Bag Game

No two days are e'er the same,
For every day, we play a game.
She hands me my brown bag, and while
She wears her Mona Lisa smile,
I say, "Farewell," and then I query her:
"Just what's in the brown bag's interior?"
Although I charm her and romance her,
She smiles, but still I get no answer.

What's in my lunch? I'll never guess.
Hearts of palm? Watercress?
English trifle or, more daring,
Sturgeon smoked or Bismarck herring?
Pomegranate? Feta cheese?
Very likely none of these.

One day, a colleague fond of gags
Deftly switched our two brown bags.
That night, what happened was incredible.
She asked, "Dear, was your repast edible?"

Of course, I said, "It was delicious."
Should I have been at all suspicious
When she turned pale and promptly fainted?
Could that brown-bag lunch have been tainted?
Could I have fantasized a plot
To help untie the marriage knot?

I'd ask my friend who got that parcel
If aught was wrong with any morsel.
That question, sadly, died aborning,
For his entire clan was deep in mourning.

So, every morning, at the door,
She'll hand me my brown bag once more.
She'll smile at me and seem so pleasant.
What's in the brown bag? Breast of pheasant?
Prosciutto, melon, spinach pie?
Radishes? Asparagi?

The question's moot, for the bag is fated,
Each day, to be incinerated.

SEX AND THE SENIOR CITIZEN

No More Omar

"A loaf of bread, a jug of wine, and thou" —
That's not a balanced diet as of now.
For Omar, it may not have been
The bread or wine that kept him thin
But the energy expended on the "thou."

Club Med

Club Med!
'Nuff said.
Wife pack bags, and she put cat out.
Blow town.
Come down.
Club Med! They have welcome mat out.

Big bash.
No cash.
Sure to be one grand vacation.
Warm sun.
Much fun.
Hedonistic population.

Great place.
Pulse race,
Eyeing all those unclad lasses.
Wine flows.
Who knows?
Maybe make a couple passes.

Cute blonde
Respond
She have six unoccupied days.
Wife frown;
Thumbs down.
Wife see twenty-twenty sideways.

Nice chest.
You guessed —
He have certain predilections.
Unwise.
Wife's eyes —
They rotate in all directions.

Man wink.
Girl think
He have cinder on his cornea.
Meanwhile,
Wife smile,
She laugh, "Well, I tried to warn ya."

Too bad.
Man sad.
He too old; no more good-lookin'.
He cry.
Wave 'bye.
He go soon back to home cookin'.

Moral:

Plain truth:
Lost youth,
Club Med give no guarantee on.
Wrong place
In case
Man decide he Ponce de León.

Gone, Those Passions Once Assailing Us

Sexual games with regularity
Now are something of a rarity.
But signs of incompatibility
Loom due to loss of our virility.

Acts we once engaged in nightly
Back when we were young and sprightly
We just talk about politely
Now that we are both unsightly.

Hormones which they call "androgynous"
Seemingly no longer lodge in us.
Wild sex parties keep on dodgin' us,
Even though we're not misogynous.

Gone, those passions once assailing us.
Gone, the Club Med ads they were mailing us.
And since our memory is failing us,
We don't even know what's ailing us.

Sex, once cause for jubilation,
Is now just dreams and contemplation.
We've reached, alas, the realization
It's on a permanent vacation.

A Look of Supplication

One day, as I was sitting, sunning, wrapped in solitude,
Indulging in just quiet contemplation,
I heard the sound of steps approaching on the gravel path,
And I saw a lady strolling toward my station.

As she approached, I rubbed my eyes. Could she have winked at me?
A dream? And yet my heart began to pound.
She walked on by. I smiled a little smile that she returned
As she let her hankie flutter to the ground.

I bent down to retrieve it — something I would come to rue —
Then I looked up at her tantalizing eyes.
A look of admiration? No, a look of supplication,
For I found that, having bent, I could not rise.

Oh, lower lumbar spine! Alas, once more you've done me dirt.
Here's a lady who could make my cares unravel,
A lady I could flirt with, one who clearly would respond.
Instead, I'm lying prostrate on the gravel.

The spinal fates are fickle. No romantic interlude.
My rendezvous is with a heating pad.
My sole companion now is just a lumbosacral brace,
As I lie and dream of what I might have had.

And So to Bed

Now that we're old and much less sprightly,
Acts we once engaged in nightly
We sample, now, in manner cursory,
About once every anniversary.

We plunge in with unbridled gusto,
With what was once a blunderbuss. Though
We still hold fast to the erotic,
A lot of it's anecdotic

Due to an ever-widening chasm
'Twixt deed and sheer enthusiasm.

Sex

Wars were fought and men have died because of sex.
Queens and chambermaids have cried because of sex.
        Tyrants have been brought to heel
        With nothing more than sex appeal,
And great men's lives have been reduced to wrecks.

A scholar or a great athlete can savor sex,
An arena where each can compete if he elects.
        In this game, only hormones count,
        Not muscles in a large amount
Or even those gigantic intellects.

For youngsters, it is not so grim, this thing called sex,
More like a workout at the gym — almost reflex.
        But several generations back,
        The kids spent less time in the sack.
The problems were decidedly complex.

To me, it never seemed quite right, regarding sex —
Those studs who could go on all night and not be wrecks.
        If it is some strange malady,
        I wish they'd pass it on to me
With, hopefully, some permanent effects.

Yet time is the eternal foe in all respects.
The earthly pleasures seem to go, including sex.
        We turn to forms of self-hypnosis
        Plus vitamins in massive doses,
With, usually, no visible effects.

Still, no one e'er gives up the ghost and still expects
Some doll will murmur yes regarding sex.
        Though oldsters are dead set on it,
        I don't think they should bet on it,
'Cause they can't remember what they should do next.

Dear Dr. Ruth

Dear Dr. Westheimer (may I call you Ruth?),
I am rapidly balding and long in the tooth.
It must be hormonal — my sex life's diminished;
My endocrine glands are apparently finished.

With such problem-solving, you seem to be expert
On TV; it's obvious you're a sexpert.
Since dalliances now tend to end in disaster,
It's time to seek help from an acknowledged master.

I met a nice lady, and I'd like to romance her,
But I fear that I couldn't take yes for an answer.
I am awfully depressed as regards this condition.
It has damaged my formerly warm disposition.

I am down in the dumps; I know just what "morose" is.
I've seen Masters and Johnson for their diagnosis.
I have tried divers techniques, and every one fails me.
Would an attitude change be of help for what ails me?

I've tried stiff upper lip, and I've tried to be placid,
But the lip was the only thing that wasn't flaccid.
So, you will be blessed with my undying gratitude
If you'll guarantee a new outlook in attitude.

Your methods may seem, to some skeptics, empirical,
But I am convinced that you'll pull off a miracle
And further your fame as a humanitarian
By stiffening . . . my resolve. Signed,

An Octogenarian

P.S.,

There is just one thing more I should say in concluding:
The attitude changes to which I'm alluding
Are not mine (my hormones are well past repairing);
It's the unhappy ladies whose beds I am sharing.

DREAMS AND NIGHTMARES

The Numbers Game

When I was a child, I was often beguiled
By visions of sugarplum fairies,
Which danced in my head as I lay in my bed,
In my own world of imaginaries.

Then puberty came. Dreams were never the same.
Each fairy gave way to a maiden,
Who danced in my head as I squirmed in my bed,
In which sanctum new thoughts were cascadin'.

Then, just as I'd reckoned, reality beckoned.
Spring's mystical rites came to pass.
And my innocent dreams went to other extremes
With most any available lass.

Now, in my later years, one same dream reappears,
Of a nocturnal tryst I held dear,
And it keeps on recurring with precision unerring,
Though embellishments creep in, each year.

This delectable dream of a dalliance supreme
Involves a young goddess I knew,
With a forty-two chest, a waist twenty at best,
And a derrière just thirty-two.

In my dream, I start reeling as I see her peeling
For the act which for years I've rehearsed.
Then I wake up in terror and discover my error —
Those figures have now been reversed!

I Wish I Were an Analyst

I wish I were an analyst,
So I could sit and listen
To patients stretched out on the couch
As they are reminiscin'.

I'd sit behind and to one side,
So they couldn't see me leering,
And take vicarious delight
At the wild tales I'd be hearing.

I'm sure that everything they'd say
Would be lewd and licentious.
I'd hang on every word, since I'm
By nature conscientious.

I'd catalogue their escapades,
Those not for attribution,
And act as their confessor,
Though I can't give absolution.

The patients' time would be well spent
To deal with their condition,
And I could send my kids to school
And pay for their tuition.

                    *   *   *

When I told this to an analyst,
He seemed a bit perplexed,
Then smiled and said, "Lie on the couch.
It's obvious you're next."

Entre Nous

Though I have not asked hitherto,
I'll tell you something, entre nous:
I'd like to have a rendezvous
And make my late debut with you.
I know it is long overdue,
Since opportunities are few,
But if I could review with you
The things I'd like to do with you,
I'd snuggle up real near with you
And nibble on each ear with you
And then get into bed with you
And simply go ahead with you.
Now that I'm getting old, it's true
There may not be much I can do,
But I could still have fun with you,
With things I should have done with you,
And though such escapades with you
Are possibly taboo with you,
There's nothing wrong with what we'd do
As long as it is entre nous.

BUT

My wife would make a big to-do.
She holds the purse strings, it is true,
And she is apt to misconstrue
The things I plan to do with you.

So if I have a date with you
And I should stay out late with you,
I hope that you are well-to-do
And your VISA card will see us through.

Letter to Mrs. Malone

My dear Mrs. Malone, could you send me a clone,
'Cause one thing is nigh indisputable:
To put it precisely, your clone would do nicely,
And nothing else would be as suitable.

Back here, I am frantic, 'cause all things romantic
Are gone from the house since you're missing.
With a clone as your double, it would be no trouble
To think it was you I am kissing.

Don't trust every word of the rumors you've heard
About the clones I'm entertaining.
Though it seems ironic, they all are platonic,
Which, doubtless, may take some explaining.

So I'll be explicit, behavior illicit
Is just not my style — that, I'm granting.
Though vows I've enacted, if your stay's protracted,
Those clones might appear more enchanting.

So, please, Mrs. Malone, I need you, not your clone,
For yours are the assets I'm proud of.
Or else send a shipment of your native equipment,
Which no one back here is endowed of.

My Dream: The Miracle of St. Bud

If I were Catholic — which I ain't —
I'd want to be the patron saint
Of the female breast — God's work of art,
Which sets the fairer sex apart.

As befits my role anent the bosom,
I'd devise assorted ways to use 'em,
Designed, of course, to help the boys
Enjoy these wondrous mobile toys.

And on St. Bud's Day, every spring,
When nature wakes each living thing,
There'd be a grand St. Bud's procession
(At least, right now, that's my impression).

My icon would be proudly borne
By nubile girls, on St. Bud's morn,
Upon their lovely, unclad shoulders,
Past crowds of gaping male beholders.

To savor this perennial sight,
The men would wait in line all night,
The youngsters dreaming of the lasses,
The oldsters polishing their glasses.

The males, succumbing to their charms,
Would gather 'round those unclad forms.
In a scene no Raphael could paint,
They'd wildly cheer their patron saint.

*   *   *

That I reached sainthood in my dreams
Is not so far-fetched as it seems.
This dream all started with a gift,
Which almost caused a family rift,

When I purchased for my shapely spouse
A Neiman-Marcus "see-through" blouse.
That was before the ERA,
Before such things were recherché.

She said, "No way! I wasn't made for it."
But then, when she learned what I paid for it,
She kissed me, saying, "That was sweet,
But may I have the sales receipt?"   .

Her motive clearly was discernible:
She wondered if that gift's returnable.
From that day on, I always chose
Other gifts than ladies' hose.

I Wish That I Were Barbara Cartland

I wish that I could write romances,
Just like Barbara Cartland,
With ménages à trois and steamy bedroom scenes.
I'd be on all the TV shows,
From Bangor, Maine, to Portland,
And be featured in the tabloid magazines.

I would write at leisure
On my eighty-five-foot yacht —
No writer's block on my deep-sea oasis,
'Cause each and every novel
Would have the selfsame plot.
All I would do is change the names and places.

Atop the *Times* bestseller lists,
I'd reach my apogee
And be up to my clavicles in pelf.
But fame and fortune, in the end,
Would not accrue to me,
'Cause I'm no Barbara Cartland, just myself.

It makes no difference how I try,
I can't write those romances.
For me, no Cartland metamorphosis.
If I could write like Barbara,
With all those big advances,
Just why would I be writing stuff like this?

Pounce de León

Palm Beach Post, 2/24/01:

> *A 94-year-old man was arrested on a charge of attempted rape, according to a Palm Beach police report. Herman C. is accused of assaulting his nurse on Wednesday, the report said. The incident happened about 11 p.m. . . . The woman said C. exposed himself . . . asked her questions of a sexual nature and attempted to lie on top of her, according to the report. C. was booked into the Palm Beach County Jail and released Thursday without bond.*

Juan Ponce de León said, "Forsooth,
I shall discover the Fountain of Youth."
We learn from his Florida journal
He was certain he'd found youth eternal.

But scientists, trained to be curious,
Have insisted his finding was spurious,
And since they've uncovered no proof,
Could it be Juan Ponce de León goofed?

The accused, in today's *Palm Beach Post*,
Could well have been de León's ghost.
The police say that one Herman C.,
Age 94, went on a spree.

Was he de León's ghost, who, in truth,
Had discovered that Fountain of Youth?
Old Herman C.'s youthful caprices
Appear to prove de León's thesis.

C. exposed himself (assuming he found it);
Then he pounced on his nurse, who, astounded,
Found him on the top and herself on the bottom —
That's the proof! *Quod erat demonstrandum!*

Samuel Cohen

Though life after death is still being debated,
I've decided to let it be known
That when I return, fully reincarnated,
I shall come back as Samuel Cohen.

In fact, it is likely that had I a voice
In selecting a name for my own,
There is no doubt at all that my very first choice
Would have been to be called Samuel Cohen.

I would have preferred it to Tavish MacTavish,
Scarlatti, or Francois Simone,
To Ivan Tovarsky or something more lavish,
Like Throckmorton Dinwiddie Sloane.

Smith, Kelly, or Jones I'd most likely eschew,
And other names just as well known.
I'd even forego Oshiburi Maru
In favor of Samuel Cohen.

                        *   *   *

I know what you're thinking: he's out of his head.
But there's no way that you could have known
That if I were he, I could jump into bed
With his luscious tidbit, Mrs. Cohen!

Love Is Sad

DREAMS AND FANTASIES

Winter

When summer's gone and winter's gloom
Fills every corner of the room,
The tropics light up in my brain,
And I dream of heading south again.

Once more, in my imagination,
I am on my annual vacation.
From all the tours I've seen while dozin',
This is the one that I have chosen:

A low-cost tour that's all-inclusive
And, yet, one which would be conducive
Of bringing, somehow, to fruition
My secret unfulfilled ambition —

A seaside inn, American plan,
Where I would be the only man,
With every beach in the vicinity
Filled with luscious femininity,

From which delectable bouquet
I'd pluck one flower for each day,
According to a well-laid scheme.
Then I wake abruptly from my dream.

Beside me, my alarm clock's calling.
The reality is too appalling.
I rub my eyes and look about me.
Those beauties have gone off without me.

And when, at last, I'm back at work —
Just another office clerk —
I blink to hide an unwept tear
And save my dreams for another year.

Dreaming

I dreamed my favorite fantasy —
That you were real and here with me.
        Just how it came about,
        I'm not aware.
I dreamed that decades had not passed,
That I had won your love, at last.
        And I awoke . . .
        And you were there.

I dreamed, one night, the telephone
Awoke me with its strident tone.
        I heard a voice,
        A voice I thought I knew.
That voice, in my dream, seemed to be
Someone I once held close to me.
        And I awoke . . .
        And it was you.

I dreamed we planned a rendezvous —
No time, no place — and yet we knew
        It was a tryst that,
        One day, we'd be keeping.
And in my dream, we would embrace,
With tears of joy upon your face.
        And I awoke . . .
        And you were weeping.

I dreamed we'd meet in some strange land
And walk for hours, hand in hand —
        The sort of dream for which
        My friends all chide me.
And in my dream, we'd consummate
The love for which we'd vowed we'd wait.
        And I awoke
        With you beside me.

Encounter

Coincidences, more and more,
Somehow led me to your door.
Were they part of a celestial plot?
Our meetings, proper and correct —
Could they have led me to expect
A dalliance in this strange, exotic spot?

Then it happened in some way.
I found myself, one sunny day,
Lying there beside you, on the sand.
Quickly, underneath the palms,
I stripped myself of all my qualms,
And caution to the winds, I grasped your hand.

Now all those fantasies I'd known
About the thought of us alone
Sprang into being yet seemed quite unreal.
My head upon your naked breast,
Our glistening bodies closely pressed —
It was just as I had dreamed that it would feel.

We laughed, we played, and, unaware,
Day turned to night. We still lay there,
Serenaded by the music of the sea.
Then, in the surf, once more, at dawn,
One last embrace, and you had gone
And left behind the sand, the palms, and me.

Strange, how encounters come and go,
Create a sparkling kind of glow,
And then retreat into your dreams again.
But we will always share that glow —
A smile, a glance, that says you know
Our dream's as real today as it was then.

Snow

It seems so very long ago
When last the land was free of snow.

Did acorns lie upon the ground?
Did fallen branches once abound?

Do I remember gopher holes
And ivy beds and verdant knolls?

Were winding gravel paths once here?
Did tiny seedlings disappear?

Did we lie — lovers — in the grass,
Amid the fallen leaves? Alas,

Were they illusions? Who can know
What dreams lie buried in the snow?

Vanessa

They told me her name was Vanessa.
I never saw her again,
Yet in my galaxy of memories,
I have seen her over and over.

She was but one of hundreds
In that huge theater foyer,
Yet I could see none but Vanessa.
Why Vanessa?

I grope for the proper words —
Aphrodite incarnate.

As she came near, she looked at me,
No, through me, as if I were not even a shadow.
Then she swept on by,
Swallowed up in the dense throng.

Why was I mesmerized by those eyes
And the tiny wrinkles at the corners?

I was certain that they smiled at me —
Not her lips, not her mouth,
Just those tiny wrinkles at the corners;
They smiled at me.

I never saw her again,
But I cannot forget
Those little wrinkles at the corners.
I know they smiled at me.

The Late, Late Show

The house is quiet.
Everything and everyone is at rest.
My eyelids are heavy, my head nods,
But I stay awake.
Once more, it is time for the late, late show.

Each night, the flickering screen
Carries me back on its magic carpet,
And my dreams of years long past
Come alive in the darkened room:

Boy meets girl; boy pursues girl;
Boy holds girl in his arms —
Every night a different star,
Each more beautiful than the last,
And each of them is you.

Suddenly I am on that screen,
Pursuing you, loving you,
But you are not in my arms.
Something is wrong here.

I must have dozed.
The room is dark.
The late, late show has ended.
The magic carpet has flown,
Carrying you, the same unattainable creature.

No matter.
There is no past.
Yesterday is today.
Tomorrow, I will press the switch,
And again you will come to me
In living color.

I will hold you in my arms,
And we will cling to each other
On the late, late show.

Neither Space nor Time

Neither space nor time
Nor the deep recesses of the mind
Are beyond your ghostly presence.

I cannot see you,
I cannot touch you,
But your ghost is everywhere.

You are beside me,
In the mystic moods of Guilin,
In the concrete forests of Vigeland.

In the snowy reaches of the Andes,
In the gardens of the Alhambra,
Your ghost surrounds me.

It sings to me in the voice of Brahms,
In the gentle phrases of Shelley,
In the soul-searching songs of Schubert,

And all, like your ghost,
Everlasting.

Let's Get Lost

It seems like years since first you said
We'd leave the world behind us
And we would steal away and hide
Where nobody would find us.

And now, our time is growing short —
No more procrastination.
I've found the perfect hideaway:
The Pennsylvania Station!

>*So let's get lost.*
>*Hordes of travelers will hide us.*
>*To each other's arms they'll guide us.*
>*And though they're standing right beside us,*
>*We'll be lost.*

>*Let's get lost.*
>*Although a thousand eyes will eye us,*
>*Crowds will hurry right on by us,*
>*And no one will identify us.*
>*We'll be lost.*

Your words were words of great desire,
So sweet that one could eat them.
But most of them remained unheard,
So I wish that you'd repeat them,

Because, though I'm not hard of hearing,
Amid this tumult and commotion,
Lost, your phrases most endearing,
Lost, your words of sweet devotion.

>*So let's get lost.*
>*Although all caution we've discarded,*
>*The din with which we'll be bombarded*
>*Will keep our secret closely guarded,*
>*And we'll be lost.*

>*Let's get lost.*
>*At last succumbing to temptation,*
>*Let's meet in perfect isolation,*
>*Right in the Pennsylvania Station.*
>*Let's get lost.*

LOVE

To Jeanne

Love is not found in baubles locked in vaults
Nor even in the magic of the bed.
Love is not being blind to other's faults,
Nor is love words, however sweetly said.

The gentle touch, returned with warm caress,
The fires that deep within each lover burn,
The silent sensing of the least distress —
Love's more than these, two lovers quickly learn.

My love for you, I see more selfishly.
It cries aloud each time we say adieu.
For then, I realize, you are part of me,
And I, no less, have been a part of you.

Anniversary

How precious is the memory
Of all the years you gave to me,
A life that could have brought you fame,
Aborted when you took my name,

A life that could have reached the summit,
You gave to me and saw it plummet,
A life of chasms, gaps and silence,
Of wandering through lonely islands.

I thank you, dearest, for your gift
Of patching each and every rift,
For your gift of lucid thinking,
For holding fast when I was sinking,

For goals you tried in vain to teach me
And for the times you could not reach me,
For all the days when you were fed up
But carried on and held your head up.

For each and every sacrifice,
God alone can set a price.
What I offer you cannot compete,
But my single gift, laid at your feet,

Is purer than the purest gold,
For you alone to have and hold:
It is my love, too oft concealed,
Which, now, before you is revealed.

The love which I hold deep inside
Is true, is real, is bona fide.
That love I give to you, in tears,
For all these many precious years.

Our Love Is like a Hurricane

Our love is like a hurricane,
A seething, turbulent affair,
                And in that storm,
                We seek its eye
To find our own contentment there.

Our love is like the desert sands
Beyond eye's reach, a sea of fire.
                There, we find,   .
                Oasis-like,
Our interludes of sweet desire.

Our love is like a river deep
That runs, unending, to the sea.
                It flows by
                Yet is ever there
And, like our love, will always be.

The Magic of the Seasons

Why is the beauty of snow's white cloak
Displayed alone in winter's chill?
Why is the murmur of spring rain
Heard but briefly in that season,
First soft,
Then silent once again?

Why do the painted tulip fields
Of Kuykendahl so quickly fade?
Why is the summer not adorned
With the polychrome of autumn leaves?

Spare me your logic irrefutable.
Spare me your astral proof —
Some master plan
That calls forsythia's golden hues
To burst forth briefly on display
And herald spring
In its own way.

You, and you alone,
Possess the magic
To turn the seasons
Inside out.

For when I dream of you
In the deep of winter,
It is spring.

Happy Birthday

My gift is not an emerald
       Or other sparkling stone.
It is something much more precious,
       Which I give to you alone.

My gift is tailor-made for you,
       The all-time-champion wife.
As you'll discover every day,
       It is guaranteed for life.

By now, you've guessed just what it is —
       It is readily discernible.
I am certain you will treasure it.
       What's more, it is returnable.

On this very special day, my gift
       Should fit you like a glove.
Forgive me if it isn't new.
       It simply is my love.

Quid pro Quo

Can there be love which leaves one without pain?
Is every loss attended by some gain?
Must every storm be followed by the sun?
For every battle lost, has one been won?
For every rose that opens to the sky,
Need there be one that withers and must die?
And must the glow with which I greet each day
Dissolve into an evening of dismay?
Must pairs of lovers realize, from the start,
The day will come when they must drift apart?
For each illusion, must one's dream be real?
Has the world of dreams and dreamers lost appeal?
Let wise men carry on their fruitless quest.
My answers lie here, cradled on your breast.

MEMORIES

The Silversword of Haleakala

At the crater's rim, my thoughts turn toward
The strange Hawaiian silversword,
A shrub on all accounts unique —
It blossoms for just one short week.
And this phenomenon appears
But once in every fifteen years.

In Haleakala's swirling mists,
No other living thing exists,
Apart from this rare cactus-flower
Endowed with a magnetic power
Compelling all who would pursue it
To scale a mountaintop to view it.

I, too, risking life and limb,
Have clambered to that crater's rim,
But unlike others who've explored
The wonders of the silversword,
To me, the candle's worth the game,
For that plant is more than just a name.

Atop that strange acropolis,
In solitude, I reminisce,
And memories return, unwilled,
Of visions which lie unfulfilled,
Faint apparitions in the haze,
From other years and other days.

And those silent plants alone can hear
My silent wish that you'd appear
And our love would flower, just as though
It did not wither long ago,
With its beauty once again restored . . .
Like the blossoms on the silversword.

silversword: a low-growing plant of the cactus family,
found only on Haleakala, a crater in Maui, Hawaii

Apparition

Again your ghost appears, and I succumb.
Again my skin grows cold, my fingers numb —
A wraith, unreal, yet I can touch your face,
And your formless being waits on my embrace.

Your apparition fades as I draw near,
Then, just as quickly, seems to reappear.
My senses warn that I have conjured you,
Yet, with the night, your ghost appears anew.

I pray sweet sleep will somehow stay the dawn
And in the darkness, you will linger on.
But in the end, if I should wake, one day,
And your ghostly figure has not gone away,

If what had been a dream becomes quite real,
What terrors would the day's harsh light reveal?
Could each of us survive that exposé,
As if the years that passed were just a day?

Would we both see the same truths others see?
And would I take that chance if offered me?
Although in darkness I reach out for you,
By daylight, you are just a ghost I knew.

The Long Ride Home

I roll up my windows,
As I've done all these years,
And my car hurries homeward,
At the close of the day.
The tires' quiet murmur
Is all that I hear
While my thoughts swirl about me,
In mad disarray,
            And I contemplate what might have been.

Those great golden visions
Which illumined each day,
The goals which, at one time,
Seemed clear and explicit —
Just how could my dreams
Have gone so far astray?
My place in the sun —
By how far did I miss it?
            And I ponder what might have been.

And I frown as I ask myself,
"Have I been cheated
By nebulous forces
Which stood in my way?"
But I know that the truth is
I could have succeeded
Had I persevered
In each task one more day.
            And I'm troubled by what might have been.

But the reverie changes,
And my spirits take wing.
Contentment envelops
Me, and I'm possessed
By pleasant reflections
Of how everything
Is an unfailing source
Of excitement and zest,
            As I think back on what might have been.

And I smile to myself
As I tote up my assets —
First, a wife, like a diamond,
One of a kind,
And our children and theirs,
Making up that gem's facets,
And our friends and good health
And our pockets well-lined —
      And I close my eyes to what might have been.

Then my mind skips, unbidden,
To the years of my youth,
To memories which,
Now, seem quite out of fashion —
The pursuit of ideals,
The search for the truth,
The frustrations of young love
And the torments of passion —
      And I smile at what might have been.

But the past is the past,
And today is today.
Life is real or unreal;
One can't have it both ways.
Young love, young ideals,
And young goals fade away
And become a mélange
From a long-buried day.
      And I weep for what might have been,

      As my car hurries homeward,
      At the close of the day.

Reality

Would anguish at a long-lost love
Burn as deep within your breast
If that lost love had never been
In time's sweet memory possessed?

Is it love or dreams that matter?
Is reality the test?
But reality is often sadder —
The lonely nights, the empty nest.

How would the dream survive the troughs
And soar on wings, up to the crest,
If, in the vague and misty past,
That love had ne'er been manifest?

Come, face the truth, for it will out,
And ardor will soon lose its zest.
Your lover is naught but a ghost,
In dreams alone to be caressed.

The Mind

The mind is a wonderful thing to behold.
It never forgets anything that it's told.
Though words seem forgotten, their time they are biding.
Like a jack-in-the-box, they pop up out of hiding.

Grandiose ideas, well worth recollecting,
Enshrouded and misty, defy resurrecting,
While yet other notions we hoped would lie dormant
Are summoned up, now, by some ghostly informant.

So many and varied, the thoughts we entomb;
One cannot predict what the mind will exhume.
And thus it occurs that my mind oft uncovers
The words that we spoke to each other as lovers.

Can it be pure chance that those words, unexpected,
Now, without warning, have been resurrected?
Words which, years past, held me fast in enslavement
Emerge fresh as raindrops awash on the pavement.

The memories of you which my mind possesses
I'd conceal if I could, in those deep, dark recesses,
But time and again — the mind is so clever —
Your face is before me, more vivid than ever.

The mind is amazing, one cannot but say,
In the manner in which it throws nothing away.

The Flame

The smallest of matches can kindle a flame,
And a spark start a fierce holocaust.
Yet, sleepless, I search through the black of each night
For one spark of the love that we lost.
Consider the fact that the tree, when it dies,
Burns hotter the longer it's dead,
But a love that grows cold will, by some paradox,
Just grow even colder, instead.

A dying fire's embers still glow on the hearth,
And a once robust blaze lingers on,
But the fires of our own love, which once burned as bright,
Are dead ashes, their warmth long since gone.

Life is reborn from the dust of those passed,
And nature, while taking, yet gives.
Though no phoenix will rise from our long-buried love,
The sweet recollection still lives.

The Swan of Tuonela

What is this hell of which men speak?
Fire and brimstone? Sheets of flame?
The ceaseless clamor of petards?
Imps in crimson leotards?
Is each man's hell, for him, unique?

A lonely swan sings a cappella,
A melancholy figure floating
On glassy waters mirrored black,
From which no image gazes back.
Is hell, for me, this Tuonela?

On those black waters, none intrude,
Save for the swan, serenely gliding,
Its sad song seeking to express
The utter, total nothingness
That permeates my solitude.

Will death compound my lonely state?
Does Tuonela draw me near?
For such as I, no resurrection,
Just waters that yield no reflection.
My hell is now; it does not wait.

Still black waters, hear my prayer.
Loose my chains of desolation.
Let my vanished lover's kiss
Draw me back from that abyss,
My soul no longer mirrored there.

Tuonela, the land of death, the hell of Finnish mythology, is
surrounded by a large river with black waters and a rapid current
on which the Swan of Tuonela floats majestically singing.

REFLECTIONS

The Fires of Autumn

Taken from a phrase in the movie The Best Man

"The fires of autumn burn more slowly"
Where, once, there was a white-hot flame,
A passion that consumed me wholly,
Its spark the mention of your name.

Our lovers' dance, our pas de deux,
With me pursuing, you demurring —
Forgotten, now. Each year renews
The fires that keep our love enduring.

The fires of young love, which burned brightly,
Linger on as glowing embers,
And I cling to you more tightly,
As our lives reach their Septembers.

An eternal story, oft retold —
Our love stays young, but we grow old.

Beside You

Nature's mother tongue is violence.
Her voice is wind and rain and sleet.
Snow alone drifts down in silence —
An endless alabaster sheet.

And when of life's long road I weary,
I think I shall be laid to rest
Beside you, on some mountain aerie,
And, by the silent snow, caressed.

Il bacio

The dream of a winter evening is a kiss,
A kiss and a kiss returned,
A pledge, a bond that breaks the silence
Of years of endless dreaming.

A kiss and another,
Each a few seconds longer,
Each preceded by a pause
To savor the treasured moments of suspenseful anticipation.

Now, like an onrushing wave that races up the sandy shore,
Then, spent, slips gently back into the sea,
Our lovers' embrace relaxes slowly. The lips now part,
And we caress each other with our eyes.

The kiss — is it the fanfare
That heralds the birth of love,
Two lives joined together,
You a part of me and I a part of you?

The dream of a winter evening is a kiss,
A fire yearning for love's consummation,
A torment without ending
The love of all loves.

Will this phantasm glow like molten lava,
White-hot, over a thousand years,
Or will time dispel the magic of the kiss
And cool the fires of our romance?

A new story, an old story,
Told by the sages, the poets, from the birth of time.
This is the dream of a winter evening —
A kiss and a kiss returned.

The Mirror

Dear friend, come join my reverie,
And my silent vigil share,
But take care, lest your deep concern
Be mirror to my dark despair.

Let questions lie unasked by choice.
Be the architect of inner peace,
Your quiet presence be your voice.
And wordless, give my rage surcease.

For this wondrous alchemy,
What treasure shall be your reward?
Perhaps, in time, to see in me
The mirror of your warm regard.

Unfinished Business

As the sleepless night drew to a close, I heard
A soft voice, gently filtered through dawn's gauze:
"Where'er you are, I'll come to you, because
We have unfinished business, long deferred."
Our eyes once touched and dared not turn away,
And our first kiss was love's ambassador.
I held you, and my arms cried out, "Encore!"
Then, suddenly, that day was yesterday,
And now, a voice says we have much to do.
Shall we unearth long-buried magic spells?
Will newer kisses equal those we knew,
Or will our meeting toll old dreams' death knells?
Unfinished business, so long overdue,
Must e'er remain unconquered citadels.

Time

Time goes, you say? Ah, no!
Alas, Time stays, we go.

— inscription by Henry Austin Dobson, on a 1922
Laredo Taft sculpture in Washington Park, Chicago

In endless queue, the silent figures blend,
Mirrored in the placid pool below,
As if those granite forms could comprehend
The poet's message, left long years ago.

We dare not look upon what lies ahead
Or grapple with events both vague and vast,
Preferring to avert our eyes, instead,
And longingly look back into the past.

In memory's soft focus, each essays
To recreate the magic of his youth,
To make the present mirror yesterdays
And its reflection somehow mask the truth.

One seeks to find the past in some strange bed,
A second looks into an upturned glass,
While others, who to Mammon's arms have fled,
Would purchase time with fortunes they amass.

But were our dreams no more than self-hypnotic?
The goals that we pursued year after year
Become a quest increasingly quixotic
And, like mirages, fade as we draw near.

Relive the past — ah, no.
Alas, just dreams remain; we go.

Outward Bound

I'm here; you are dead.
God's will, they all said.
I suffered and bled,
And you died instead.

You're gone; I remain.
You rest; I feel pain.
Will years bleach the stain
Of being your Cain?

Good friend, underground,
Have my ears now found
That requiem's sound?
Am I outward bound?

Does my time draw near
To Hell's dark frontier?
Is this, then, my fear,
That we meet, this year?

My days nearly spent,
Now filled with death's scent.
Are these hours meant
To repent, to repent?

As night and day blend,
My hand I'll extend
In love, my old friend,
And join you in the end.

Epilogue

Skinny-dippin'

It's twelve o'clock or thereabouts.
"The party's dying!" someone shouts.
"Everybody in the pool!"
The voice is gay; the words are cruel.

My mind goes back so many years —
The eager innocence, the fears —
Cavorting in the buff, the sight
Of moonlit bodies in the night.

In little groups, young figures hovered
And, with a gentle touch, discovered
The magic of the other gender
And the wonderment of their surrender.

What painful blows the years have dealt
To bodies once so young and svelte,
Revealed as each of us undresses,
Hidden in the pool's recesses.

Every year, we play the game
Of pretending everything's the same,
Of casting off each decade's yoke,
Of escaping nature's morbid joke.

Can night conceal the uniformity
Of the crime of age and its enormity?
It's pointless to be self-tormenting,
But nature is so unrelenting.

Though you must accept what you can't alter,
The onslaught of the years will falter
If you shun despair. Just rise above it.
Come join the party. You will love it.

If your *joie de vivre* retains its flavor,
Then the night is young; it's yours to savor.
Let your psyche be your shield and armor.
Jump in the pool. You'll soon feel warmer.

Just close your eyes. You're back in school —
"Everybody in the pool!"

Biographical Note

Born in 1915 in St. Louis, Missouri, Ben Milder is the author of more than one thousand poems of light verse, written over the past forty years. In 1979, his book *The Fine Art of Prescribing Glasses Without Making a Spectacle of Yourself* won the American Medical Writers Association's Best New Book of the Year Award (sometimes called the "Pulitzer Prize for medical texts"). Ben Milder's light verse has been published in many magazines and journals, including the *Palm Beach Post*, *Milwaukee Sentinel*, *St. Louis Post-Dispatch*, *The Critic*, *Long Island Night Life*, *Light*, and the *Journal of Irreproducible Results*, as well as in the anthology *The Best of Medical Humor*. Professor Emeritus of Ophthalmology at Washington University School of Medicine, Dr. Milder resides in St. Louis with his wife, Jeanne.

Other Poetry and Short Fictions Available from Time Being Books

EDWARD BOCCIA

No Matter How Good the Light Is: Poems by a Painter

LOUIS DANIEL BRODSKY

You Can't Go Back, Exactly
The Thorough Earth
Four and Twenty Blackbirds Soaring
Mississippi Vistas: Volume One of *A Mississippi Trilogy*
Falling from Heaven: Holocaust Poems of a Jew and a Gentile *(Brodsky and Heyen)*
Forever, for Now: Poems for a Later Love
Mistress Mississippi: Volume Three of *A Mississippi Trilogy*
A Gleam in the Eye: Poems for a First Baby
Gestapo Crows: Holocaust Poems
The Capital Café: Poems of Redneck, U.S.A.
Disappearing in Mississippi Latitudes: Volume Two of *A Mississippi Trilogy*
Paper-Whites for Lady Jane: Poems of a Midlife Love Affair
The Complete Poems of Louis Daniel Brodsky: Volume One, 1963–1967
Three Early Books of Poems by Louis Daniel Brodsky, 1967–1969: *The Easy Philosopher*, *"A Hard Coming of It" and Other Poems*, and *The Foul Rag-and-Bone Shop*
The Eleventh Lost Tribe: Poems of the Holocaust
Toward the Torah, Soaring: Poems of the Renascence of Faith
Yellow Bricks *(short fictions)*
Catchin' the Drift o' the Draft *(short fictions)*
This Here's a Merica *(short fictions)*
Voice Within the Void: Poems of *Homo supinus*
Leaky Tubs *(short fictions)*
Shadow War: A Poetic Chronicle of September 11 and Beyond, Volume One
The Complete Poems of Louis Daniel Brodsky: Volume Two, 1967–1976
Shadow War: A Poetic Chronicle of September 11 and Beyond, Volume Two
Shadow War: A Poetic Chronicle of September 11 and Beyond, Volume Three
Shadow War: A Poetic Chronicle of September 11 and Beyond, Volume Four
Shadow War: A Poetic Chronicle of September 11 and Beyond, Volume Five

HARRY JAMES CARGAS *(editor)*

Telling the Tale: A Tribute to Elie Wiesel on the Occasion of His 65th Birthday — Essays, Reflections, and Poems

JUDITH CHALMER

Out of History's Junk Jar: Poems of a Mixed Inheritance

(800) 331-6605

http://www.timebeing.com

GERALD EARLY
How the War in the Streets Is Won: Poems on the Quest of Love and Faith

GARY FINCKE
Blood Ties: Working-Class Poems

ALBERT GOLDBARTH
A Lineage of Ragpickers, Songpluckers, Elegiasts & Jewelers: Selected Poems
  of Jewish Family Life, 1973–1995

ROBERT HAMBLIN
From the Ground Up: Poems of One Southerner's Passage to Adulthood

WILLIAM HEYEN
Erika: Poems of the Holocaust
Falling from Heaven: Holocaust Poems of a Jew and a Gentile *(Brodsky and Heyen)*
Pterodactyl Rose: Poems of Ecology
Ribbons: The Gulf War — A Poem
The Host: Selected Poems, 1965–1990

TED HIRSCHFIELD
German Requiem: Poems of the War and the Atonement of a Third Reich Child

VIRGINIA V. JAMES HLAVSA
Waking October Leaves: Reanimations by a Small-Town Girl

RODGER KAMENETZ
The Missing Jew: New and Selected Poems
Stuck: Poems Midlife

NORBERT KRAPF
Somewhere in Southern Indiana: Poems of Midwestern Origins
Blue-Eyed Grass: Poems of Germany

ADRIAN C. LOUIS
Blood Thirsty Savages

(800) 331-6605

http://www.timebeing.com

LEO LUKE MARCELLO

Nothing Grows in One Place Forever: Poems of a Sicilian American

GARDNER McFALL

The Pilot's Daughter

JOSEPH MEREDITH

Hunter's Moon: Poems from Boyhood to Manhood

BEN MILDER

The Good Book Says . . . : Light Verse to Illuminate the Old Testament
The Good Book Also Says . . . : Numerous Humorous Poems Inspired by the
  New Testament

CHARLES MUÑOZ

Fragments of a Myth: Modern Poems on Ancient Themes

JOSEPH STANTON

Imaginary Museum: Poems on Art